Textile with Birds and Smoke

To Sal'
Wonderful to
meet you,
Best wishes
Ken Tulupn.

ALSO BY KERI FINLAYSON

Rooms

Keri Finlayson

Textile with
Birds and Smoke

Shearsman Books

First published in the United Kingdom in 2026 by
Shearsman Books
P O Box 4239
Swindon
SN3 9FN

Shearsman Books Ltd Registered Office
30–31 St. James Place, Mangotsfield, Bristol BS16 9JB
(this address not for correspondence)

www.shearsman.com

ISBN 978-1-83738-015-2

Textile with Birds and Smoke

CONTENTS

For Alan, as always.

As a teenager I was very ill. For five years, pain was something I balanced carefully and gently inside me. I read the few books of poetry I had repeatedly. I read constantly. I listened to birds from my bedroom window and I thought about the things that flowed around the island of my bed. I had my final operation at seventeen. At eighteen I left for university to read theology. Though not a theist, isolation and pain had gifted a deep fascination with the contradictions of contemplative life.

The concerns that were born during these years have grown with me over a lifetime.

Prints

A wire footed wren has been here.
It hooked a chain between the seams
then followed it. Look at the stitch:
light, cuneiform cuts in the snow.

Tangled with chirrup and fruit

On a breakneck of rocks
Tangled with chirrup and fruit,
Froth, flute, fin, and quill
—Dylan Thomas

And in those years
it was always late November - bare
dove grey, then darker: woollen must and briefly surfacing light.
And in those years I pinned the days
with shapes of trees and mostly this one:
Wind smeared, toppling
with the toppling wall; a stagger and a yearn for the long horizon;
spined and hard with berries little more than stones made crimson with
       a shine,
but mostly made soft with birds that changed the whole blurred thorny smear
to panicked song as I walked past to school.

I didn't have the words until I was fully grown.
The stones, the birds, the panicked spines,
I found them in a book which quietly had kept for me
that briefly surfacing shine: the long and lit horizon
of the calm and waiting line.

Hysteroplastic

Hysteroplasty: reconstructive surgery used to repair a malformed uterus where layers of stitches are used to create a normal shape.

Trapunto: a quilting technique using two layers, the underside of which is slit and padded producing a raised surface.

I have five scars
Three long slices
And a diagonal cut on the right side of my abdomen
with a nick above like the morning star

The pain arrived the second time I bled
twisting through a place
lower than my rumbling stomach lower
than nervous flutterings or queasy flips
through an inside I didn't know I had
I was thirteen

I bought two metres of calico
a pad of polyester batting
and imagined myself a skirt
with a drop waisted panel
trapunto quilting – a thickened yoke
running from hip to hip.

Thirteen, learning the mad extent
of my family's poverty
wrapping my gussets
with thin sheets

of cloudy loo roll

I drew a double trail
interwoven lines centre bowed
to such complexity across the yoke
it took me days to figure the
clustered knot
that would dip below.

'This is what it is,' men
with stethoscopes said
dry screams no tears
only new brand new vowels
cried below audibility

a difficulty with button holes and
insertions
a zip is beyond impossible
how on earth do you stop a gape
when you have no means to measure?

Fourteen; appendectomy
fifteen: removal of fallopian tube
sixteen: pain
seventeen: pain
seventeen: pain

the weight of gathered fabric pulls
teenage hand stitching into
little frilled puckers dragging out
gaps so you might see my thigh
or my holed nylon tights. Sew tighter.

Pain makes a new space:
a streak of grey prairie
under slow prickling
tv static sky
one day it turned inside out

a light kapok ball all strands
all threads and air
thumb and finger rolls
I stuffed the over-under tracks
and sewed up the wispy slits.

A new space:
a wand rubbed over cold gel
the inside out on a screen
and o! the faces
a room of white coats

an irregular pentagon of thick quilting
from navel to ilium to pubis
holds up the whole world as a skirt
watch the raised lines run in
mad, mad looping.

The tailor's slice
showed a second, blind
blooded womb.
A cervix
snipped
his stitch
unfixed
the floor turned red

the weight of fabric pulled.

Tacking ripped
the surgeon threw the old bag on the floor
worked a rolled hem
embroidered it with woven lines
little looping mad-frilled puckers
of fleshy threads and air.

The stitching in my centre
doesn't show
but o how long, how long now
I've known
how the weight
of gathered fabric pulls
the over-under knot
that's always there
the interwoven lines

of fleshy threads and air.

Assisted Dying Debate

A pro-Atropos argument:

It is both dangerous and rude to snatch scissors.

Gulls

We know them don't we

                                    gulls.

Solid bodied, white. The beak a split scream.
Yelping us up a storm or a turned tip.
Seeding our sky like weeds.
They are not souls or prayers
but whole cathedrals of rage.
Feathered vaults, gathering all known sound and pitching it as noise
against the false horizon.

Our bodies are inadequately boned for such wrath.
Richly dense they lack the cavities for height.
We open our mouths and bleed long strands of gravity.
Our speech the opposite of flight.

Factory Second

For David Holah and Stevie Stewart

Stevie,

I was fifteen in 1985 and hadn't had newness for years.
Tugging through crazed piles in jumble sales
I made a god of second hand and prayed hard
for burgundy jumbo cord
an almost knee-length knit or
a quilted batwing sleeve.

David,

The hobby farm across the wall from us
was owned by one who saw the lack next door.
Her husband ran a shed of Cornish girls
stitching hems for Katherine Hamnet
and the rims of cuffs and holes for you.
And when the bolts of cloth were bad or
some girl's hand had failed a seam
the next-door woman came to me
with caste-off cloth and cones of thread.

Often of an evening
the nest of dials and wire that
crouched in our front room
would grind and clunk
and all the light would disappear –
no 50ps – and no point looking.

So I re-sewed your seams by candle light
licking threads and peer-poking through
the silver patterned elastane blend
stretched tight across my palm.

No money: no magazines
no TOTP, no i-D
no Face, no NME
no music, no club, no scene
often no money to get the bus to school.
But o! the shape of those low dipped hems!
those cuffs!
those unexpected holes!
showing me that I might move out and up
that all I needed was a good drape
a slight stretch and an unexpected cut.

Bedspread 1984

beneath stitched ditches   verges   greensward satin edges
the nylon scent of pink will lift you up and pull you under

spread you   lay you flat

the pepper tongues   the green joints

of

campion   foxglove   willowherb
ragged robin   dog rose   vetch

     so sleep
     and let the low heat rise
     through loose stones and that tightest sound
     thin insects wound to meet your eye

beneath diamonded woods   groves   fenced off copses the
thermoplastic fat of blue will lift you up and pull you under
spread you   lay you flat
the busting stems   the almost poison of
bluebell   harebell   periwinkle
hyacinth   cornflower   sage

     so sleep
     you know these weeds
     the differences of roots and bulbs
     their gummed exchanges as all saps breathe

beneath fields   pastures   overlocked meadows
the polymeric drift of yellow will lift you up and pull you under
spread you   lay you flat
the milky tubes   the false stars of
primrose   celandine   trefoil
dandelion   aconite   weld

so sleep
you know that you will find
no other things like these
the weight of fabric
the run of thread the scald of colour
and-the-by and-the-with and-the-constant-
from
of your endlessly
flowering breath

Mitten Hands

I am six years old
and I know that because there is snow today
there may be wolves
and I must wear red.
My hands are placed in the mittens my grandmother made.
The scarlet, wool-acrylic blend
saves my thumbs from my fingers
and, threaded through my stiff plastic mac,
the long bleed of crochet stitched to the red ribs
keeps me in a slack crucifixion.
I scrape cold white feathers into my flat hand.
The knit one –
purl one fibres that have been flung through a multihued spinneret
and coagulated in sodium thiocyanate hold the crystals up as rills of fluff.
I hold up my palm and offer it to myself as if I am my own nervous horse.
Protein-lipid strands, pushed through the follicles of a bleating sheep
slowly absorb the melt until
water finds its way
and my hands get wet.
I'm cold and numb and restrained
and I know that when I am finally unstrung
my hands will be red.

Red as
the mittens
Red as
the cloak
Red as
the wolf's tongue
Red as
the woodsman's axe
Red as
the grandmother's
unstrung
gaping
throat.

Hero Dress

Stitching Marlowe's Hero and Leander with found words from the ME+EM website.

for Breeze Barrington

She bought a hero dress that pulled its weight,
One that took her from desk to dinner, lunch 'til late.

> *The outside of her garments were of lawn,*
> *The lining purple silk, with gilt stars drawn;*

A warm weather hero: trans-seasonal, versatile
Breathable and lightweight, in a timeless style.

> *Her wide sleeves green, and border'd with a grove,*
> *Where Venus in her naked glory strove*
> *To please the careless and disdainful eyes*
> *Of proud Adonis, that before her lies;*

She purchased occasion wear dressing with polished functionality;
A contemporary hero piece that flattered, formally.

> *Her kirtle blue, whereon was many a stain,*
> *Made with the blood of wretched lovers slain.*

It was an everyday hero, a one-stop solution;
Luxury that would last, in colourful iterations.

> *Upon her head she ware a myrtle wreath,*
> *From whence her veil reach'd to the ground beneath;*

She bought the hero dress that we all need,

Her veil was artificial flowers and leaves,

One that will give us endless, effortless outfit-building ease, one

whose workmanship both man and beast deceives.

A Portrait

after Robert Graves' 'The Portrait'

I have a cloak
that lets me walk along the highroad
invisible at noon.
It's lined with children's chub and spit
And trimmed with forks and spoons.

Fuzzy Felt

Of the many things I think childhood might be
my favourite
is a box of Fuzzy Felt.

A hand, smooth and small picks out and up
a shape, perhaps a square
places it on the waiting black.
And then, three more
smaller, red – windows
and a door.

And there we are: childhood.
These shapes, pre-cut, approximate
stuck, unstuck
blank, unfilled
are moved, removed
until this scopic, fuzzy world's
been willed.

S/S A/W

Spring
Hyacinths. That bright, wet scent.
She is fifteen and growing through
herself. And o! that new blue
dress, as light as it is
unspeakable.

Summer

A cotton smocked belly top and denim cut offs
in the supermarket beyond
the ring road. Her gloss-tipped toes
brush the fraying raffia.

Autumn

The first of endless years of heathery tweed,
tartan, and *velvet's new jewel tones.*
Her first suede ankle boot.
Her first military button.

Winter

A loose mauve knit in a gauzy
blend of mohair and silk
like her first mistletoe kiss –
so soft an itch.

Purkinje Silk Shift

Purkinje Shift: the tendency of the luminance sensitivity of the eye to shift
towards the blue end of the colour spectrum at low illumination levels.

the end of november   a forest

each day   long before sunrise
I walk to a hut by the edge of a lake

the forest is quiet and dark
the hut is hexagonal and small

this is where I spend short days
making straight lines from that unlit place
to the balanced surface on my lap

                          I should be writing
                          instead I stitch

the forest is quiet and dark
the hut is hexagonal and small

               november in the forest sees the sun set at four
        at half past   it's almost dark

I stitch this forest with my back to the lake the setting sun
the static day

     and then

          dusk dips
                   a
                   n
                   d

          ten centuries of purplish
          shed needles cross-hatch to such depth
          that the give in each step is an endless

                  listless

                                          crash

branch gaps smoke up like glass

pine turns to

lines of birch

swinging from hyacinth to pitch

a
n
d

            dusk dips and we stitch

            ten centuries of purplish
            shed needles that cross-hatch to such depth
            that the give in the thread is an endless

                  listless crash

                  a
                  n
                  d

                  we are in a forest

                  losing the sky

                  days fracture

                  long before sunset

we walk through the flat screen
to the smooth silk

this is where we sew
the short days
we should be writing

    the forest
    fabric and
    page

  breaks quiet
    branches
    the quiet and balancing branches
    into
    blue
    a
    n
    d
    darkening

    sewn and written

    listless

    november

    trees

Cold Water Swimming

At fifty

oestrogen drops – the sap's

slid – so I'll slipskin – the ebbing-waning salt

wash that gave my eyes brimfulls – after one last sea-storm –

has dried like high-blown weed – so I'll slipskin

Surfaces – lifted from slack muscles – have

softened and now that I am glossed

with new whiskers and

buoyant with new

fat I'll

slipskin

Look at me in the water

Look at me bobbing in my bobble hat and false flippers

Look at the wet weed brushing my true thighs – the silky-selkie fluid

inside

outside   inside

Dorothy Becky Scarlett

1979, I ask my sad mother
if she was in black and white
when she was young.
If she wore a skirt
like softened slate.
If she wore a moonish
leg o' mutton blouse
smoked with runs
of flinty buttons.
If her eyes were always ash.

My sad mother brings out
a pair of shoes as red   as
a polka-dotted dress as gold   as
and a soft heap of velvet as green   as

explaining that before she had been born
Dorothy Gale skipped her slippers   down
Becky Sharp slipped into the arms   of
and Scarlett O'Hara tilted her chin   in
Technicolor's three strip process
so that as a child, her then and far
was in colour.
It was her now and here that was noir.

Opus Anglicanum

Head caught in the trap of a
too-tight roll neck
my free eye
catches a look in the long mirror:

Thighs pale from a season
in M&S pointelle thermals
stomach paunched over never-best pants
I am one of the Bayeux Tapestry's
slaughtered thegns
laying at the end of the linen
looting myself with a struggle
as the story peters out.

Back along the
long bank of the Embroidery
where bare Norman legs
flinch into the late summer sea,
boats are loaded with hauberks
hung on poles like racks
of T-shirts bound for the back
of a budget retail chain store.

Perhaps Odo's nuns in loose-necked robes
stitched those legs, that mail, those boats
with woad-dyed wool
in runs of split and stem
filling space with pads of couch
praying that no man's pricks would again
unpick the sinew from the skin.

Nuns whose needles made the tale
of things unmade by sword and lance
whose needles prequeled the loss
of forest taken from all hands
whose needles painted beasts
transformed from meat to game
whose open throats sang there and then
for men in blood-soaked chain.

Nuns whose open throats sing here and now
as I stand before the long glass
struggling in the strangling grasp
of my bargain Shein roll neck
in a cotton-elastane blend.

Writing objects

Tanizaki, comparing the writing brush
to the fountain pen, argued that if

the Japanese had invented the latter
then it would have had a tufted end – like a bird

An end, perhaps, like that of the
Senkaku albatross, the bird that draws

up phials of brine to ink out on
islands across the East China Sea

Though it was not a pen, but
Hayakawa's mechanical pencil

that brought new shapes to the painted page
a cuteness that carved gaps of thin white air

between archipelagos of script

It has been said that this very fineness
encouraged the young to fill the void

between their words with fat hearts and full faced smiles
an adolescent plea perhaps to pebble

those white and widening seas
with the babbling signs of infancy

I think that white between our words, my love
is death, and writing objects

But you and I should rest
And let the white sea spread

We should let the distance stay un-pebbled
and we should let it be far

And we should let that single
quiet and spanning, cloud-crowned bird

Now carry us from shore to shore

Ding Dong Bell

"…spectators, including kings and queens, shrieked with laughter as the animals,
howling with pain, were singed, roasted, and finally carbonized."
Norman Davis, *Europe A History.*

Puss
Cat
Puss
Cat
Puss
Cat

Johnny Thin:

The hinged mouth is a perfect yawning orchid.
Just look at that small tongue. It's such a firm petal.
And the teeth? Rows of little beaks.

If you lower them by the bagful into the fire
You can contemplate the yowl.
Note the changes in register from singe to char.

They can also be strung up and emptied for their strings.
Here we can deal with the paws. Peeling is good.
Though of course they would be voiceless throughout.

Johnny Stout:

Mine's now found sprawled on my wife's bed or
snugged in her lap. It's not that I'm cuckolded by this cat.
We all love those plush, upholstered bones.

I have commissioned portraits. The cat has been
positioned on silk cushions with dishes of thick milk.
Look how the light soaks her to the skin.

And we always gather round as she opens herself to us.
O that dip between ear and skull.
O that long palmful of spine.

Puss
Cat
Puss
Cat
Puss
Cat

Where we once put her in now we pull her out
From Johnny Thins to Johnny Stouts.

Just imagine, though, that warm heart.
Trilling in your mouth.

Well

they fell as carbonized lumps
became silk tied
public-domestic
footloose-hearth bound

blind pawed

taking our sleep, yowling with sex
marrying the master's daughter
sleeping in her bed
circling her lap
getting the cream

in boots.

So, we move from Johnny Thin to Johnny Stout
pushing them in and pulling them pulling them out
stripping them for strings

giving them the top of the milk
for such needy independence.

Beast fable puppet.
Strutting Chanticleer.
Rentier cat.

Soft sheaths
held up like hooks.
A gesture and a tool
to act on the tugged reel
and concertinaed paper
the failing mouse and
the dragging bird.

All wells.

Twenty Lambert and Butler

Time thickens and slows to anchor.
Two men and one woman sit.
There is no street audience
But from the bar they are all scene:
Bill and May stage left;
Joe and the cigarette machine stage right.

Above their heads are object heavy shelves:
Books, jugs, patterned plates.
No brasses.

Three brown pints are being drunk.
One is angled to the lips.
Two stand flat.

Time has slowed to smoke.

Breath slips from loose lips.

At first, pale wisps of plosives peep and retreat
until whole white sentences ready to be launched,
then out sails what Joe would and wouldn't.

Each word escapes its berth, shoots straight
becomes all centre, all edge, all curl.
Streaming past the tipped and tipping glasses,
they float up to meet Bill's first white syllables
as they push off hard.

His coulds and couldn'ts gain speed,
spread round table tops and table legs,
first flat, then frilling. Turning in and in as
rilled pirouettes.
The feathers curling back and back;

a dance of curlicues and reels;
drifts of sinkings and risings.

Slowly May inhales the long strands of shoulds
and lets out a cirrus of skimming shalls
that navigate the stone islands of the ashtray,
the glove,
the glass,
the mat,
the slumping, open bag.

Book Scent

varies according to date.

The first eighth of the second shelf
to the right of my fireplace
gives this:

Basic Tap Dancing, Diana Washbourne, 1979

base note:	peach rayon nightie
heart note:	milk bottle rim
top notet	ripped switch

Political Thought 1848–1914, Ernest Barker, 1942

base note:	undersink
heart note:	cider foam
top note:	Queen Anne's lace

Horrible Histories, Terry Deary, 1999

base note:	chewed cuff
heart note:	post office queue top
top note:	neck

Misogynies, Joan Smith, 1993

base note:	warm stem
heart note:	edged blanket
top note:	fresh suds and stale pepper

Patriot Poems for the Young, SS Tait, 1915

base note:	bell clash and cutlery
heart note:	gravel freeze
top note:	tip of cloddy spade

The Baldwin Primer, Mary Kirk, 1899

base note: wet leaves and liquorice
heart note: lead stub
top note: throat-back after tears

Collapse Vol VII, Negarestani and Mackay, 2011

base note: coagulate emulsion
heart note: skim of bleach
top note: cups

Galata Glass

for S.B

You said you saw the street made Christmas with the shine
of broken things that split the light –
of objects cut and loosed before their time.

Lamp making Beyoğlu streets unwind
through coloured glass and hammered wire.
You said you saw these streets made Christmas with the shine;

that small ponds and balanced bones inside
your head had thickened with the thickened air, now twice
as dense with objects cut and loosed before their time.

The street had grown from site to sight
a lengthening of the world so bright
you said you saw the street made Christmas with the shine

and you had grown from I to eye
a lengthening of the vowel so slight, pulled by
the weight of objects cut and loosed before their time.

And now, despite
the lack of lamps, night after glassy night,
you say you see that street made Christmas with the shine
of objects cut and loosed before their time.

The Storm Outside

Anna, the last time we met I thought how beautiful you were
small as a bird, your cheek bones high and slanting.
I remembered how, the previous spring, while waiting in the narthex

of St Peter's for you to catch your breath
we watched the sparrows tilt between the statues
of Constantine and Charlemagne.

It was there I told you about Bede's sparrow who, exiting
the storm outside, darted through the long house
slanting in loops above the heads of men to tilt on breath

as dry as fire. Anna, those men in that long room
when compared to birds, sit as still as the statues
of Charlemagne and Constantine

and that the sparrow has to stir up such storms to keep itself
in flight: a frantic drum of hollow bones slanted
to panic through the warm, still house.

It is so much effort to stay above slow breath.
But the storm outside is movement
wild winds and full, wet air slanting as rain.

And Anna, the storm outside is movement; on it
and in it you will tilt beyond all house and home.
Anna, the storm outside is movement

on it and in it you will rest and rise
rest and rise
like an emperor.

Speaking about the Henge

We stopped and parked then
strict as wings
the jackdaws threw their sound against the stones.
It ricocheted as lines of glass
as shining tricks of triple k.
The stones sent back the sound as stings of song
that broke the sun to spokes
that spoke the day, or was it year?
Anyway, a calendar of sun and throat, ofsunandthroat
hung here.

        At the interactive museum and shop
        we learned that before the henge
        a tangle of dense oak had spread across the downs.

        How broad those branches must have been
        with leaves as constellations of light and sap
        in miles of lacing arcs that tracked the sun.

We learned that forests are green weight

                        held

by the gravity of song
that they are

                        folds

of budding stars, spiralling and lobed

                        fixed

by the voice of blackbirds
in the clarity of groves.

We were walking back towards the car when

lax as wings

a blackbird spilt its song over the grass.

It worked the paradox of light and voice
that deals with flight and weight's dense curse
and when it was as sure as stones it looped a course
above our heads and gently took the sun apart.

Our guidebook said that blackbirds ranged in woods
and these were gone; that trees were howked by spades of bone
to clear a space for time's new hoax and what
was left were tricks of stone: the uprights aping oaks.

We learned that at this place of slash and burn

event was made

an uptight marking of place and turn.

That song, chakkked from the necks of daws, prisms.

That this was a site of lithic modernism.

Gossip

From Flushing, Falmouth rose up like a wave.
I rode the jogging foot plate of the pram
along the tow path as it broadened into street
and hardened at the very end as cottages.

Rows of false and distant aunts lived here,
in two-up two-downs cut by open stairs
where front rooms were rag-matted and hard-chaired,
and back rooms were stone-wet and almost yard.

These cooked-up aunts gathered in that smeechy back
to crouch between their tea-cupped teas,
tonguing tight shapes, rocking themselves joyful with spite
and the shared electricity of unkind words.

Powerless, powerful, nylon-pinneyed
school friends of my Nan, they clotted the world
with their making breath, thickening it up until
from their lips a steam of mouthed men rose.

And there before my saucering eyes
another village was tongued to life
animated by animosity.
Inconstant. Told low motives clothing it.
No better than it ought to be.

Plush

Thinking I might, despite my many years,
be looking a little *wild child*
a little *Courtney Love*,
I giggled wildly when told that
that night, in my faux fur coat,
 I looked like Nookie Bear.

Finding that I was inhabiting the skin
of a 1970s TV puppet
I was mindful of my googling eyes,
my rigid, hinging jaw.
And to maintain my own voice
throughout the evening
I made sure I avoided laps.

What it must have been to dress in pelts
of animals who'd had blood and bone.
A two-fox stole perhaps, a pair of glassy
eyes resting on each breast.
The wearer must have had such a taste
for rabbit and for bins.

Or what it was to trail long mink coats
gifted by demanding men.
All those languid thirties starlets
with a sudden urge to grab a fish
and gut it.

And then, and then, a 1960s Susan
in A-line astrakhan
swinging a score of silky lamb pelts
a score of foetal lamb pelts
as she twisted and she bleated
into the bloody, motherless air.

A History of Swanskin

When I first saw the word   Swanskin
it brought to mind Grimm's nettle shirt
the one that had been thrown over the
last of the long-missed six brothers.

That shirt   with its unfinished sleeve
had left the poor boy with a swan's wing

a swanwing
a swanskin

 an armful of white feathers.

Cloth made from nettle fibre
glows green under its white.
That sixth brother must have looked like

         Spring under snow.

This swanskin the one I'm thinking of now is made from
fleece not feather

wool not wood-weed.

It's not grown from dabbled up fishlings
frogspawn
or river greens.

This swanskin is
grass and clover made
sheep mouth and belly made.

Swanskin, a woollen cloth made in Dorset until the late nineteenth century, was fulled with West Country clay and napped by West Country teasels. It is

thick and
>   white and white
>   and waterproof.

Few examples of it still exist outside
the work of experimental textile archaeologists.

The Peace of Utrecht
>   the balancing of ropes and pulleys
>   frozen to voices inked to the white
>   gave Newfoundland's
>   pale lichen and dark spruce
>   black rocks and long shore
>   to the British.

>   Settlement and trade grew fast
>   Dorset men came to work the water.

>   Cold Wessex bodies wrapped in swanskin jackets.
>   Hoods rimmed with rime.
>   Hands hooking cod.

Dorset men stayed North to hunt.
Cold Wessex snow-stung hands inside swanskin mitts
until sleeves were flung back as the gun was raised to a whitecoat
or a Black Duck.

Boats-that-left-Poole-looped-north-towards-
Newfoundland-with-salt-for-salting-
the-schooners-swung-south-to-Portugal-
with-salted-cod-returning-to-
harbour-with-salt-and-wine-
salt-salting-salted-salt-
wool-white-salt-white-
cod-white-wave-white-

on that outward journey
schooners ballasted themselves
with soil dug from the clay vales

that sweep between
the-white-lines-
the-white-lines-
the-white-lines-

of Dorset chalk and limestone.

I have read two things:

the first is that in a museum on Change Island, Newfoundland,
there is a pair of swanskin mittens;

the second is that in Harts Cove, Twillingate Island, Newfoundland,
there is a garden made from tipped ballast.
If you look at a map you will see that between Twillingate and Change
Island lies New World Island.
This rock stretches itself out in streaks of skerries.

They are named:

Cobbs Arm   Toogood Arm   Pike's Arm
                         Herring Neck

I've decided that that patch of tipped ballast grows nettles.
I've decided that there is not enough stem to spin to a shirt.
I've decided that there is just enough stem for a sleeve to throw over three arms and a neck.

I've decided there is just enough stem to glow green under all that white.

Hemming

April. D drags her skirts through Grasmere Lanes.
Wet hems carrying from C to W from W to C:

A sudden downpour.
Glass drops among the green.
Celandines slicked to suns.

Birdsong after the rain,
after the risen breeze had
sunk like again like celandines.

The gleam of elms,
half-born leaves sticky
with their own nativity.

A soldier, brain looping
back to battles like the
buttons on his frock coat.

A robin threading its
red through the last
of the rose hips.

A mossed stone
churched by branches.
A lane lit by stars.

D shakes out her skirts and spreads them to the fire.

Tells W that

'The moon shone like herrings in water'

Tells C of

'the unutterable darkness of the sky.'

Boundary Layer

Scalar fluxes from urban street canyons. Part I: Laboratory simulation
(Janet F. Barlow, Ian N. Harman and Stephen E. Belcher, 2004)

Abstract

1

Flow over urban surfaces depends on surface morphology and interaction with
the boundary layer above.

Janet, this city you built limits
itself and
splits to
one canyon.

> Smoke: Dove and screen snow.
> River to rivulet to stream.
> Always alive with-up.

2

However, the effect of the flow on scalar fluxes is hard to quantify.

Really Janet, this city you built displaces
replaces.
Blocks to
secret gullies.

> Smoke? Hold up your hand.
> All those fortune telling whorls?
> Useless.

3

The naphthalene sublimation technique was used to quantify scalar fluxes out of a street canyon under neutral conditions.

Janet, this city you built offers
up tracks of
clean blocks stacked
to street.

Stretch further then keep still.
Curl those tips over the lintel.
Tilt your chin so that your mouth
gapes to the sky.

4

For an array of eight canyons with aspect ratio H/W = 0.75, increased flux was observed in the first 2-3 canyons for moderate and low roughness upstream.

Janet, this city you built blocks
flows then
trains them
like vine.

Fog is rolling in.
Low roughness you say?
Must be a pea-souper.

5

This is consistent with predictions of the length scale for initial adjustment of flow to an urban canopy.

Janet, you stoop to your streets.
Quick breath, slow breath.
Shallow-deep
Blow.

Wind blow.
Nudge the soft lamp light drip.
And carry footfall on up to

6

The flux was constant after the initial adjustment region and thus dependent only on local geometry.

Janet,
youthinkred
youthinkplastic
youthinksmooth

Chimneys stump angles
and smudge
footfall joins and runs
runs along.

7

For a street canyon in the "equilibrium" part of the array, each facet of the street canyon was coated with naphthalene to simulate scalar release from street, walls and roof,

Janet,

you stoop to your street
coat each block
with flicks of naphthalene.

Smoke licks it all.
Picks up the dinner

scrape.

The sudden sneeze.

8

Fluxes from the roof and downstream wall were considerably larger than fluxes from the street and upstream wall and only the flux from the downstream wall exhibited a simple decrease with H/W.

Janet,

look hard.
See the muddle.
See the warming colours in this fist of plasticine.

Footfall, knife

scrape.

Sneeze.

9

This suggests that flow decelerates around the recirculation region in the lee of the upstream building, i.e. a recirculating jet rather than a symmetrical vortex.

Janet,

look hard.
See it slow.
Spin
 again.

Spin
again.

Footfall knife-scrape.
Sneeze footfall knife
scrape sneeze again! Footfall
knife-scrape sneeze!

10

The addition of a second source within the street canyon resulted in reduced fluxes from each facet for H/W > 0.25 due to increased concentration of naphthalene in the canyon air.

Janet

it all thickens and

then it all

the smoke the sneeze the knife-scrape

the smoke the sneeze the knife-scrape

the footfall

slows

it all

slows.

Things-out-of-Themselves
(On seeing the work of Katy Moran at the Tate, St Ives)

Look out there

those gulls contain their flight within themselves
knowing what is body and what's beyond
and can, with this awareness of shape and form,
perch and dip as branches take their bow.

And

that beach, scooped and patted to packed shape
as turrets, ramparts, crenels and small moats,
it's strung to watch the slow, ablating line
as smelted and smoothed rock returns to smoke.

Through here

these statues, struck from stone and struck as stone,
as thigh, as throat, as brow, as heel, as nape,
they're taking shape and making known
pressing back the pressing world
standing and holding their own.

And

this sound, slipping like a moonstruck song,
child-cry dipped through gull-scream yearning
up and down from whoop to wave
like rose-weeping-seeking Columbine.

Now, in this room

these pictures held in rigid frames
holding things that lift from lines and slide
so all our objects' limits are in doubt
and my shaky heart steps up into my mouth.

Assisted Dying Debate

An anti-Lachesis argument:

With the advent of flexible laminated tape,
we can take our own measurements.

Lambs and how they live

Sometimes as mouths
and sometimes as legs.
Green jawed, leaking sap
letting the milk spill from your warm wrist
to that soft crook as you tug the bottle back.

> *sing:* *Those spine tied, stilt frail spouts*
> *that toe tip to your small tremors?*
> *They'll catch your flails before*
> *bucking them out.*

And sometimes as fleece
and sometimes as flesh.
In twists by wire twists
gold pale and streak greased
soaked with lanolin then dried hedge-crisp.

> *sing:* *Now lift and loose the lemoned skin*
> *to show the meat that's*
> *carved pink-thin.*

But mostly as blood and mostly as voice –
a bleat of hyssop flung from the vein
s/lung across the firmament
with Bos, Marys and Dames
to be daubed on lintels, painted on frames.

> *sing:* *Lambs live as a herbed soteriology.*
> *A sharp scented, heart bleating*
> *death-living savoury.*

Lambs: and how they live

as mouths:

        slit like hooves

as legs:

        green boned

as flesh:

        open to influence

as fleece:

        in twists by wire twists

as blood:

        hyssop and door

(see, see how it streams in the firmament!)

as voice: Eloi!

as song

as rhymes read

as lost

as found

as easily led.

Anchorhold

Anchorite: A male recluse
Anchorhold: A place of withdrawal
Anchoress: The feminine ending

Anchorites withdraw from the world in order to offer up prayers to it.

During the Middle Ages women who chose this consecrated life were attached by stone to the body of their church.

Walled into a small cell[1] they devoted their lives to prayer and to the contemplation of their god.

An anchoress' enclosure often contained an open grave enabling her to be in constant contemplation of her own mortality.

Some anchoresses would, each day, scrape a little earth from the floor in order to make this pit: their own final hold.[2]

---

[1] An anchorhold, the dwelling place of an anchorite or anchoress
        a pocket
        a blind cave
        built onto the outer wall of a church or a monastery.
Across the medieval period, appearing as
        lean-to shacks
        timber accretions
        strapped to square-towered Norman churches
        like barnacles on the rock of the church.

[2] In 1505 the anchoress Margaret White's enclosure was preceded by a mass.
        Processed in prayers and psalms
        I
        choose death over voices in gardens
        over voices carried to roof lines
        over voices heard through doorways
        over voices exchanged over gateposts
        over your voices.
        All of them.

The thirteenth century *Ancrene Riwle* likens these anchoresses to birds.

Such as

the pelican[3] who has little flesh and many feathers.

So little flesh and so many feathers.
Help me shed these feathers as I fall.
Until I am lace.
My bones a run of threads that hold my shape.

So little flesh in which to dip my beak.
With which to make these feathers red.
O I have spoken and spoken out of turn.

I would tend to silence but it is hard.

---

[3] Believed to pierce the flesh of its own breast in order to nourish its young, the pelican's red-tipped sword-beak rests modestly on its white.

The Physiologus, a second-century bestiary of unknown authorship, says:

it is an exceeding lover of its young. If the pelican brings forth young and the little ones grow, they take to striking their parents in the face. The parents, however, hitting back kill their young ones and then, moved by compassion, they weep over them for three days, lamenting over tho blood itself awakens them from death.

The writer of the Riwle, advises the 'testy anchoress,'

to make her mouth
the sword-bill of the pelican.
Confession is to draw blood.
Her blood is to scribe brief reanimations – to scribe refleshings.
Little stabs of bloody life as she lowers herself to dust.

From the first bloody
                    womb-freed yelp   breath is a long fall.
                    A cadence that begins in air
                    and ends in earth.[4]

                    In this hold I'll count the shallows 'rise until I'm held

                    O I would tend to silence   but it is hard.

---

[4] Withdrawing, descending sisters in Christ died twice:

        as they crossed from the social to the solitary
        and then as they crossed from flesh to bone.
Even in death, an anchoress' flesh wouldn't leave her space.
Excavations of anchorholds reveal bones beneath the floor.
At St Annes Church in Lewes the anchoress, in her second death, was laid in the
spot where she had knelt,

                    the spot where her eyes had been allowed
                    a view of the altar through the hagioscope

                                            or squint.

The *Ancrene Riwle* instructs the anchoress not to 'handle herself too gently.' Gentle handling, it says, leads to self-deception. Purity is to be found in mortification of the flesh, in pain, and in fasting.

Such as

> the ostrich[5] who has so much flesh
> that its feet will always drag the earth.

So much flesh that I think that I will never leave the earth.
Help me loose these stones by heaping more.
Help me loose these stones until I've lost
this thigh, this throat, this brow, this heel, this prickling nape.

> So much flesh that I drag the earth.
> I want to bear this weight until I'm

walled.

> I would tend to lightness but it is hard.

'For the body is clad in the cloth
and the flesh in the skin,
and the bones in the flesh
and the heart in the whole.'

Not heart   light breath is found inside the whole.

---

[5] The anchoress who is like an ostrich is not bird enough.

The ostrich is of dubious breeding. Many ancient and medieval scholars believed the ostrich to be a product of cross breeding: an unhappy combination of camel and fowl.

Poor unspiritual, leaden ostrich: too coarse   too fleshy   too heavy.

Aristotle thought that some of the ostrich's organs were those of a bird, others those of a quadruped, most likely a camel. With its head and neck more hair than feather, and its seemingly cloven feet and ample breast meat, its repulsive feet drag the earth. For the author of the *Ancrene Riwle*, mammalian, fleshy sin is not to be emulated.

O I would tend to lightness[6]   but it is hard.

The anchoress is told to contemplate the suffering of Christ, likening him to the jewel agate. The *Riwle* says that by contemplating his suffering the poison of sin can be driven from the heart.

Such as

the eagle[7] who hides the precious jewel inside her nest.

That precious jewel inside my nest.

I will make myself a nest of thickening thorns

until I am thinned   soft enough to

hold

---

[6] Anchoresses were drawn from all strata of society.
A few were of poor origins and there are records of some aristocratic women who sought enclosure.

Most anchoresses appear to have wanted to leave the seemingly comfortable, middling, genteel swathe of medieval English life to embrace a living death.

> *To leave the scent of warm lavender.*
> *To leave the slow work of the quick needle.*
> *To leave the lightness of dry linen.*
> *To leave the gleam of the waxed table.*
> *To leave the hip-weight of the key.*

[7] The writer of the *Riwle*, in triple simile, tells the anchoress to be like the eagle.

  • Her heart is to be like the eagle's nest.
  • She is to think of her Christ as if he were the jewel agate.
  • She is herself both the bird and the nest.

Medical mythology tells us that the eagle-stone, sometimes an agate, sometimes an aetite, is a powerful protective against poison and a profound generative force. As well as protecting the nest from the venomous snakes, it was thought without these stones the eggs of eagles would not hatch.

to anchor this stoney child inside.[8]
Wall me so that I am inside out

and outside in. A thorn-soft nest to hold the

agate stone.

I would tend to lack but it is hard.

His flesh is torn and drenched with stings of blood
so that his heart is tender beyond touch
He shows me   and I dip   my fingers in
and find there is   no sense   in the mildness of this

void.

O I would tend to   lack but it is hard.

---

[8] Pliny the Elder in his Natural History tells us:

This stone has the quality also, in a manner, of being pregnant, for when shaken, another stone is heard to rattle within, just as though it were enclosed in its womb; it has no medical properties, however, except immediately after it has been taken from the nest.

Recommending attaching them to pregnant women or cattle to prevent spontaneous abortion, Pliny goes on to warn against wearing them for too long.

Such is their power, they may cause prolapse. Quick!

An anchorhold was often built with two windows: one that allowed a viewing of the church's altar, the other, much smaller, affording a sighting of sky.

The anchoress is encouraged to be not only like the solitary pelican but also like a night bird, perhaps the owl,[9] a bird who leaves the house at night to feed.

Such as the owl

the night bird who leaves the ruined cell to score the desert sky.[10]

Night sky   feed me   heavenly night let
the sharp cuts of light   your white   thorn-slits
split my tongue.

---

[9] The *Riwle* exhorts the anchoress to seek nourishment for her soul during the night. It likens her to the owl who lives in secrecy and finds its food in darkness.

It says, *'the night fowl' in the eaves betokeneth the recluse who dwells under the eaves of the church.'*

The recluse, her heart-nest tucked into the body of the church, is asked to be a private creature, contemplating, praying and seeking 'night nourishment for her soul.'

[10] Night nourishment, flight in darkness, knowledge in the sight of a starry heaven, Minerva's wisdom.

                                   Minerva stands centre.
To her east, wisdom comes from darkness   death   ruin.

Symbols of destruction bringers of bad luck, owls of the desert are wisdom as touched by death, wisdom from the coldness of stars and wisdom from the closeness of ghosts.

Palestinian folklore tells us that owls are bad luck.

In Bedouin culture owls are the spirits of vengeful warriors.

The Middle East gives us owls that are the souls of the unavenged. Psalms 22:6 mourns: *I am like a desert owl, like an owl among the ruins. I lie awake; I have become like a bird alone on a roof.*

Job 30:28-29 howls: *'I went mourning without the sun: I stood up, and I cried in the congregation. I am a brother to dragons and a companion to owls.*

We can score each other with our wings.
We can score each other with our wounds.

From my window I will see the stars and
from my window I will see His simplest star.
Two gaps in stone that let me bleed out prayer.

I would tend to heaven but it is hard.

Night, He says, is what He calls secrecy
and night can be at any time of day.[11]
I can fly from eye and ear   walled
yet open to the glitt'ring sky.

O I would tend to heaven   but it is hard.

The anchoress is warned against idle chatter. Though she may be allowed
to advise other women who visit the window of her cell she should, for the
most part, be like the sparrow: alone under the eaves, twittering prayers for
a world while hidden from it.[12]

Such as

---

[11] To Minerva's north, her bird is Blodeuwedd the betrayer, banished to the night,
her flower face haunting the dark woods. In Scottish folklore she is the Katyogle,
harbinger of death.

In the English 12th century poem, 'The Owl and the Nightingale', owl seated
on his ivy bough, argues that his own deathly cry incites man to repent his sin.

Even when killed and strung as a scarecrow, even when his ghoulish face and
ghastly feathers are spread like a cross in the fields, owl is doing a service: protecting
coming crops, warding off the blacker birds.

[12] The *Riwle* speaks of another bird that rests under the roof of the church – the
sparrow.

It takes pains to make clear that this is not the sparrow of the flock or the
sparrow of the fields
- This is the single sparrow.
- The anchoress is to be *'a lonely sparrow under a roof.'*
- She is to keep a vigil for the world.

the single sparrow spilling song[13]

spun with breath and shaped

through holds.

I sink

and I sink

I would tend to stone but it is hard.

O I would tend to stone but it is hard.

A single, watchful sparrow, perhaps Bede's, flying fast through the Great Hall.

A bird-soul momentarily lit by hearths, by laughter, then out fast into pagan darkness. Psalm 123 sings: *our soul has been delivered as a sparrow out of the snare of the fowlers*

That single sparrow shooting through the long house, out of the fowler's snare is also sacred to Aphrodite. Sappho tells us in a fragment as brief as the flight through the Hall that the goddesses' chariot is drawn sparrows.

Lascivious little things, Chaucer in the *Canterbury Tales*, describes his Summoner as, as hot and as lecherous as one.

[13] The author of the *Riwle* writes that the sparrow, *Hath yet another property which is good for an anchoress, although it is hated: the falling sickness.'*

- The falling sickness is said to be the sparrow's infirmity.
- The anchoress must disregard, mistreat, neglect her body.
- She must let herself fall to the earth, preventing the corruption of pride.

The lustful bird-as-soul should tumble from heaven.
But there is, says Hamlet, *'special providence in the fall of a sparrow.'*
How glorious. How glorious for the anchoress to fall to the scraped earth alone.

Assisted Dying Debate

In the face of Clotho, I am ambivalent.
Faced with cloth I am.
Faced with cloth, I am.

Acknowledgements

Thanks are due to the editors of *Shearsman* magazine, *Poetry Wales* and the *Brain of Forgetting* where some of these poems have previously appeared. Three of the works have been exhibited as visual poems: 'Anchorhold' at the 2023 Folklore Society Conference in St Albans Cathedral; 'Bedspread 1984' at the 2023 Textus exhibition at The Torriano Meeting House, London; 'Cold Water Swimmer' and 'Mitten Hands' at the conference, *Fairy Tale Trouble* organised by the Cambridge Centre for Research in the Arts, Social Sciences and Humanities in 2025.

Further thanks to Alison Winch for camaraderie and conversation, to Tom Goldman for serendipitous research assistance and to Janet Barlow, Ian Harman and Steve Belcher for the use of their words in *Boundary Layer*.

www.ingramcontent.com/pod-product-compliance
Ingram Content Group UK Ltd.
Pitfield, Milton Keynes, MK11 3LW, UK
UKHW012320221225
466348UK00002B/119